THE ROLE OF THE FRONTAL LOBE IN TODAY'S SOCIETY

The brain and decision making

RAFAEL ANTONIO VARGAS VARGAS

DEDICATION

To my family, for their unwavering support and encouragement throughout all the projects and challenges I have undertaken in my life.

CONTENTS

FOREWORD

The frontal lobe is one of the most important structures of the human brain and plays a fundamental role in decision-making and individual behavior. Its full function is reached in adulthood, and for this reason, the study of the development of the frontal lobe in the early years of life is a topic of great importance, as it can have implications for the mental well-being and potential of each individual.

As we advance in understanding the brain, especially the frontal lobe and its influence on society, we know its role not only in everyday life but also in more complex societal issues, including politics, economics, and ethics. These issues are closely linked to the capacity of individuals in society to make decisions.

Additionally, because the maturation of the frontal lobe depends on the individual's experiences and interactions with their environment and peers, which begin at birth, education—which depends on the family, community, and educational system—is crucial for its proper development. This has not been adequately considered due to the existing gap between education and the research and knowledge that neurosciences have about the frontal lobe, its development, and function.

In today's society, the frontal lobe is increasingly influenced by external factors such as family, society, economy, culture, and technology, among others. According to published scientific evidence, these factors can sometimes positively influence its development, while in other cases, they may have a negative effect.

This book will explore these topics without claiming to cover all issues related to the frontal lobe, offering a unique and integrated perspective for non-expert readers on the role of the brain in today's society and how we can use this information to improve our lives and our world.

THE AUTHOR

THE FRONTAL LOBE AND ITS IMPORTANCE

"[Neurons are] cells of delicate and elegant shapes, the mysterious butterflies of the soul, whose fluttering wings who knows whether they will one day elucidate the secret of mental life."

Santiago Ramón y Cajal.

Spanish neuroscientist.

The frontal lobe is essential for the proper functioning of today's society, as it is related to the ability of human beings to think critically and make appropriate decisions when faced with particular situations or problems. It is also important for self-control and the ability to regulate emotions and behaviors. Without a mature and functional frontal lobe, it would be difficult for individuals in a social group to interact properly with each other and to take part effectively in society. To achieve these functions, the lobe has specific and essential structures and connections that determine its particular functions.

Frontal lobe structure

The frontal lobe is a part of the brain found in the anterior part of the skull, it communicates with all areas of the brain either directly or indirectly. It receives information from primary and secondary sensory areas and especially from association areas. It also connects with areas that control emotions such as the limbic system and areas that control vital functions in the hypothalamus and brain stem. It makes bidirectional connections with movement control areas, which are areas that it influences to set up movement patterns that determine behavior. These connections do not exist at birth and are established and modified throughout life due to biological and environmental factors that stimulate on the one hand the formation of myelin in neurons, a process called myelination dependent on the presence of glial cells called oligodendrocytes, and on the other hand the formation of contacts between neurons, a process called synaptogenesis. In this first stage of formation, heredity is fundamental, but also adequate nutrition, since carbohydrates are required to generate energy, lipids for membrane and myelin formation and proteins to form new proteins and the chemical substances that act in the synapse, the neurotransmitters, many of which are formed from essential amino acids obtained from the diet. Similarly, early sensory stimulation is necessary to stimulate neural circuit formation. Myelination is a sign of brain maturation, the first areas to myelinate are the primary sensory and motor areas in the first years of life, and the frontal lobe is the last structure to myelinate.

Frontal lobe functions

The frontal lobe manages many of the brain's most complex functions, such as decision-making, task planning and organization, judgment, critical thinking, abstract thinking and reasoning. It is also involved in the regulation of behavior and emotions.

Complex brain functions are supported by simpler brain

processes that include attention, visual, auditory, spatial and motor memory, and the ability to associate information from multiple sources. Based on these processes, the individual can respond to stimuli coming from his environment in an adequate way to interact with his environment, adapt and/or change it according to his needs. This ability to interpret reality and act according to the stimuli received from the environment is acquired progressively and depends on an adequate psychomotor development, which in turn depends on biological factors such as genes, nutrition, state of health and non-biological factors that are determined by the environment and the stimuli received: family, media, community, educational system. Of all the brain structures, the frontal lobe is the structure that reaches its maturity late, at the end of adolescence, but this depends on the progressive and summative acquisition of processes that are developed throughout childhood and adolescence. In this sense, environmental factors and experience are key to this maturation. The brain and especially the frontal lobe continue to develop and change, thanks to experience and social interaction until well into adulthood, at which time aging-related processes may decrease the brain's ability to modify and adapt to the demands of the environment so that some abilities may diminish under normal conditions.

Frontal lobe and emotions

The frontal lobe plays a crucial role in the progressive development of important skills, such as problem-solving and decision-making abilities. It is also closely associated with an individual's capacity for emotional regulation and control. However, these regulatory abilities, which are initially minimal or absent in the early stages of life, are acquired gradually and in a sequential manner. For instance, control over emotional behaviors is limited during the early stages of life, but as children and adolescents mature, their frontal lobe becomes progressively more effective and efficient in performing these functions.

Frontal lobe and reasoning

The frontal lobes of the brain are related to decision-making and executive function. In the scientific literature, these two processes are often presented as an aspect derived from the acquisition of simple brain skills such as attention, motivation, memory, learning, which lead to the development of other skills such as making comparisons, analysis, making judgments that ultimately lead to other skills including organization, planning and creativity among others. The frontal lobes of the brain manage aspects associated with intelligence, as their activity allows the individual to set and achieve goals, prioritize tasks and make rational decisions. But what does this mean in everyday life? If a person is not fully aware of what is happening internally (needs) and does not adequately relate it to elements and phenomena in his environment (risks, threats), he can make wrong decisions that can have dire consequences and put at risk his life or his economic and/or social well-being, as well as that of the individuals around him, whether family, community or society.

Determinants of rationality

The proper development of the frontal lobe is influenced by multiple factors including biological factors such as genetics and non-biological factors such as environment and experiences. For example, children with genetic alterations of several types (trisomies, monosomies, among others) may have as clinical manifestations delayed psychomotor development and children who are exposed to a stimulating and enriching environment may have a more developed frontal lobe than those who do not have such stimuli.

Frontal lobe damage can affect a person's ability to control his or her behavior and emotions. For example, a person with frontal lobe damage may have difficulty inhibiting inappropriate or impulsive behaviors and thus have difficulty regulating their emotions. They may also have difficulty making decisions or solving problems.

Importance of the frontal lobe

In today's society, where there are more demands and permanent external stimuli, it is important to take care of the frontal lobe and keep it in good condition. This includes exercising regularly, getting enough sleep, eating a healthy diet and reducing stress. It is also important to challenge our mind and keep it active through activities such as solving puzzles or learning new things.

In summary, the frontal lobe is an essential part of the brain and decides the rationality of the individual, which is essential for the proper functioning of today's society. For this reason, it is important to stimulate its maturation, take care of it and keep it in good condition so that individuals can take part effectively in society and participate rationally by making informed decisions.

References.

Interested reader are encouraged to review the following documents.

- Rosselli, M. (2003). Brain maturation and cognitive development. Revista Latinoamericana de Ciencias Sociales, Niñez y Juventud, 1(1), 125-144.

- Vaidya, A. R., & Fellows, L. K. (2020). Under construction: ventral and lateral frontal lobe contributions to value-based decision-making and learning. F1000Research, 9.

- ARDILA, Alfredo. Executive functions brain functional system. In Dysexecutive syndromes. Springer, Cham, 2019. p. 29-41.

- Hika, B., & Al Khalili, Y. (2021). Neuroanatomy, Prefrontal Association Cortex. In StatPearls [Internet]. StatPearls Publishing.

UNCOVERING THE FRONTAL LOBE: A CASE HISTORY

"Flexibility, resilience, and uncertainty, that kind of adventure, are in our nervous system, they are part of life."

Oliver Sacks.

American neurologist.

T here are many arguments and evidence supporting the role of the frontal lobe as the structure responsible for higher mental activities. Some evidence is the result of experimental work and others are historical reconstructions of clinical cases. One of the most famous historical cases was reconstructed by Dr. Antonio Damasio. Antonio Damasio is a Portuguese neurophysiologist specialized in the frontal lobe. He immersed himself in the study of the frontal lobe, even resorting to recreating historical cases. The most famous case dates back to the late 19th century. It is the story of an American railroad worker, Phineas Gage, who injured his frontal lobe in a work accident after a steel bar pierced his skull in the left orbitofrontal region. Although he survived, after the accident, the man was no longer the same, his personality and temperament changed rapidly. From a responsible, respectful, polite man in general, he became a carefree, vulgar, aggressive man. He showed little respect for his colleagues, did not accept rules or restrictions, was stubborn when contradicted, and although he was capable of thinking about future goals, he could not judge the risks involved and was incapable of long-term planning, he simply survived from day to day. He was inconsistent and easily gave up on assignments and quit jobs. He made bad decisions that caused him to fail in every project he started. This and other cases, coupled with various experimental studies, suggest that there is a relationship between emotions, social interaction, decision making and executive thinking. The latter, executive thinking, is the determinant of an individual's constant and continuous actions to obtain a goal and includes the ability to plan, execute, self-evaluate and correct errors. Until this moment it was considered that the brain and especially the cerebral cortex did not have a specific function, but with the behavioral changes that occurred in Phineas Gage after the accident and the specific lesion in the frontal region, it was suggested that in the brain there are areas in charge of functions such as planning, organization, social interaction, morality and others that determine emotional aspects such as joy, sadness, anger, fury, which in many occasions are regulated by the individual according to the environment. The scientific evidence later obtained supports the hypothesis that the full development of the frontal lobes is essential for an individual's ability to judge, reason, make introspections, control emotions, plan and predict risks, respect the rules of the game and norms. This development depends on many biological, temporal and experiential factors, and the experiences depend on the interaction of the individual with his or her family, social, educational and cultural environment. In other words, for the acquisition of mental maturity and rational ability, constant contact with our environment is essential.

References.

Interested reader are encouraged to review the following documents.

- McHale, L. (2022). The Curious Case of Phineas Gage. In Neuroscience for Organizational Communication (pp. 29-34). Palgrave Macmillan, Singapore.

- Sevmez, F., Adanir, S. S., & Ince, R. (2020). Legendary name of neuroscience: Phineas Gage (1823-1860). Child's Nervous System, 1-2.

- Fellows, L. K. (2019). The functions of the frontal lobes: Evidence from patients with focal brain damage. Handbook of clinical neurology, 163, 19-34.

THE FRONTAL LOBE IS A CHANGING STRUCTURE

"Everything we do, every thought we've ever had is produced by the human brain. But exactly how it works remains one of the greatest unsolved mysteries, and it seems that the more we investigate its secrets, the more surprises we find."

Neil deGrasse Tyson.

American astrophysicist.

The brain has the ability to adapt and change dramatically in response to experience, a process known as plasticity. The frontal lobe is uniquely flexible and capable of undergoing significant changes in response to experience and learning. For example, research has shown that learning new skills or engaging in mentally stimulating activities can lead to changes in the circuitry that shape frontal lobe structure and function. These changes can improve cognitive function and increase the brain's ability to perform tasks. Frontal lobe plasticity is not limited to childhood and adolescence. It can also occur in adults, allowing for continued learning and development throughout life.

In general, the frontal lobe is a very plastic part of the brain, capable of undergoing significant changes in response to experiences and learning. These changes can improve cognitive function and increase the brain's ability to perform tasks.

The frontal lobe, plasticity and the enriched environment

A topic of research in recent years in neuroscience has been the environment rich in sensory stimuli (visual, tactile, acoustic, olfactory) and its role in brain maturation processes (technically brain plasticity, including processes related to the maturation of brain circuits related to memory and learning). It has been shown that a stimulus-rich environment for experimental mice, stimuli including wheels, colors, obstacles, etc., in their cages helps them learn faster than mice living in boxes with few or fewer objects. This means that the world around us determines our brain development, and this world includes the one that surrounds us in intrauterine life, up to the world after birth and that accompanies us until old age: this enriched environment includes food, stress, physical activity, education, recreation, housing, environment, among others, and are necessary for the correct development of the central nervous system, especially the frontal lobe.

Biological and non-biological factors are fundamental for a harmonious development of the frontal lobe or for altering its function. In prenatal development, biological factors are determinant, and this includes maternal nutrition, emotional well-being of the mother, non-use of addictive drugs, prenatal control by health systems in order to check normal embryo-fetal development and detect risk factors that threaten this development: infections, toxics, maternal diseases, etc. In postnatal life both biological and non-biological factors interact to figure out brain development and both factors are important. During childhood and adolescence, adequate nutrition is fundamental, but non-biological factors are also essential, including social factors such as a balanced family environment, family income, quality education, health care, and opportunities for recreation and leisure. In other words, the environment is a key factor in creating enriched environmental conditions that stimulate brain development and maturation, which will decide the formation of rational citizens. Family, media, education, social institutions, create part of this enriched environment that are probably molding the man of today and of the future.

Given this, many questions arise, some are related to the family environment and how it can be a determinant of frontal lobe development. For example, some questions are: what can we expect from Third World countries or developing countries, where problems such as maternal and child malnutrition, teenage pregnancy, single mothers, displacements and migrations especially of women and children in vulnerable conditions are common phenomena? What can we expect from developing countries, where misery or poverty levels are close to 50%? What can we expect in Third World or developing countries, where maternal and child health services are inaccessible or reserved for the elite, or urban population and marginalized populations or rural populations are unprotected or have inadequate quality social security services? What can we expect in Third World or developing countries with limited access to quality education in rural areas and displaced populations? What can we expect in a world where family breakdown, domestic abuse and family, gender and social violence in general are permanent stress-generating phenomena?

The family environment is one of the determinants of the external environment that stimulates brain development, but in addition to the family environment are other factors that are the order of the day and that every day play a relevant role, these elements of the environment to which few individuals can escape are the media. The next question is then in relation to the media. Since childhood we are exposed to radio, television, press, cinema and nowadays to information coming from the Internet. In the face of this, the questions revolve around this: are the media aware of this responsibility when they create an enriched environment full of false values (exaltation of life and easy wealth, exaltation of artificial beauty, exaltation of the path of least effort) and where social values such as respect, tolerance, discipline, honesty, respect for rules are condemned or ridiculed? Cinema, radio, television and press are constantly at the limit of what is socially acceptable and what is ethically unacceptable, sometimes shielded by the right to information (does the right to inform allow the manipulation of information according to particular interests?) and to show reality (should the total reality be shown or only the one that sells and guarantees ratings?) These audiovisual stimuli are the ones that permanently bombard the individual, stimulate his brain maturation and lead him to rely on this information at a given moment to make decisions in daily life such as buying a good, a service, expressing an opinion or in sporadic actions in which, through a vote, he makes decisions that can influence the community.

Another topic of debate related to this enriched environment that directly stimulates the maturation of the frontal lobe is related to education. We live in a world of transition between the classical education of classroom, teacher and board and new educational proposals, among them "virtual" education supported by communication and computer technologies, a proposal that was forcibly accepted due to the compulsory confinement derived from the COVID-19 pandemic. As in any time of transition, adjustments can create chaos and damage the generation undergoing such changes. In many cases the transition may require longer or shorter periods of time, multiple adjustments and ongoing evaluations to measure results, which has not been the case in recent years. That is why several questions arise regarding the education provided today, among which are the following: Does education encourage the individual to assume criteria of commitment and responsibility with himself and his environment?; Does current education promote high levels of demand that stimulate brain plasticity and therefore the maturation of the frontal lobe? Is it more important in education the form (complying with indicators and statistics) or the content (level of training and mastery of knowledge) that reflect and favor brain maturation?; is it more important the way education is provided (technological resources, pedagogical methods) or the content of what is provided?; Who should define the level of demand of education, the individual who receives education (who is often called the client) or society, represented by educational institutions and teachers, who should demand minimum technical and professional requirements of high level that guarantee a future development of the individual in a society that is part of a globalized world that has challenges and demands?; Are the educational institutions convinced of their social function or are they only seen as mercantilist institutions that fulfill lucrative, statistical and financial objectives (income and expenses, money, students, teachers), disguised with indicators of quality standards?

And finally, other elements that are part of this enriched environment are the social institutions: governmental, religious, military. All of them are made up of individuals, normal human beings, with virtues and defects, but who stand for society and who, being in positions of leadership, become models to follow. However, it is common nowadays to see scandals of all kinds in many of these institutions where individuals behave in ways that border on antisocial behavior by acting against the general interest and in favor of personal interests. Other questions then arise: are the members of these institutions (political, religious, military) authentic representatives of society; is society aware, when it chooses, of whom it chooses; should society assume the responsibility and consequences of its representatives? Many of these representatives and many of these institutions become role models for present and future generations. The attitudes, behaviors, words, thoughts of institutional authorities are engrams that permeate the collective unconscious and somehow transform society positively (Mahatma Gandi, Nelson Mandela) or negatively (Adolf Hitler, Idi Amin). The welfare of a nation, its development, its present and future human capital depends to a great extent on its leaders. If there is no welfare, the result is a society with unsatisfied needs, non-conformity that can lead to political and non-political violence. In this sense, scenarios can be created in which a premature child, the son of an adolescent mother, the product of gender violence, malnourished, who during his postnatal life sees his relatives murdered or witnesses family or social violence, whose education comes from television, public schools and his friends, but who may also be the victim of public officials (military, religious, teachers, etc.) may be receiving a trauma as severe as that of Phineas Gage. In adulthood this individual will not have an adequate rational thinking ability, which added to hundreds of thousands of other individuals probably explains why many nations fail to achieve adequate and sustainable human development over time.

Poverty, malnutrition and brain plasticity

Poverty is a problem that implies social inequality and affects both developed and undeveloped countries. In the first case, in developed countries, there are levels of misery and poverty that generally affect migrants and native but socially excluded people. In undeveloped countries, where misery and poverty are more accentuated and widespread, people in conditions of misery and poverty increase as a result of various phenomena including accelerated urbanization processes, violence of various kinds, but often affecting rural populations, forcing entire communities to move to urban areas, where they will feed the poverty strata on the periphery of the large metropolises. These migrants are joined by the unemployed and people excluded and discriminated against for several reasons (race, gender, drug use, etc.). All those who are affected by misery and poverty lack the minimum living conditions and opportunities to develop as individuals and contribute to society. This becomes a vicious circle that prevents social advancement, as it contributes to keeping the same social conditions through generations, which is to say, it prevents the progress of these individuals, their families and the community.

Many of these elements present in the condition of poverty

have a negative impact on brain development, but one of the most determining factors is inadequate nutrition during the prenatal and infant stages, because it is during this period that the brain achieves its maximum development. Malnutrition can be either protein malnutrition, secondary to a diet with minimal protein intake, or protein-calorie malnutrition, secondary to minimal (or non-existent) food intake.

Since the late 1960s some researchers studied the effect of malnutrition on cognitive task performance in rodents. They saw that rats raised on a poor diet performed poorly on memory tasks. But, interestingly, this appeared before structural brain damage was present. The characteristic was that the rodents had low energy, were not highly active and therefore had little movement and their interaction with the surrounding environment was minimal and they ended up isolating themselves. The researchers then concluded that a low-calorie diet reduced the animal's motor activity, its interaction with the environment and thus its ability to perform learning tasks. In the 1970s, the Guatemala project was developed in which researchers evaluated the impact of a protein-supplemented diet in children. The protein was added to a part of breakfast, atole (a beverage prepared with corn). The result of this research showed that adding a protein supplement to the diet, in addition to reducing infant mortality, improved growth rates and improved performance on cognitive tests. But this improvement in these tests was only clear if it was associated with schooling. In other words, nutrition alone or schooling alone are not 100% determinants of cognitive ability, but if both elements are added together, school performance improves notably, especially in children of the age group where the risk of malnutrition is extremely high.

Other studies showed that eating school breakfast regularly had a positive impact on children's cognitive ability. An added study showed that anemia had a negative impact on the development of children's motor and cognitive skills. In these cases, an iron-supplemented diet improved the ability of anemic children.

All these studies show that poverty affects children's overall development, which is reflected in short stature, low weight, anemia, low immunity, isolation, lethargy and finally psychomotor development disorders. This psychomotor retardation is probably due in the initial phase to an insufficient caloric intake that reduces neuronal activity and thus the child's exploratory motor activity and its ability to interact with the environment, which is ultimately the necessary stimulus for normal brain development. In the long term, the deficit of proteins, calories, vitamins, trace elements, among others, in the diet affects the processes of brain plasticity, a critical process in the first years of life, which includes: neurogenesis or formation of new neurons, especially in the prenatal phase, synaptogenesis or formation of synaptic contacts between neurons. Synaptogenesis is a necessary process in postnatal life for the creation, maturation and continuous remodeling of key neural circuits in processes such as memory, learning, visual and spatial recognition, among others.

In an environment of extreme poverty and in addition to malnutrition, the child not only lacks adequate food, but also lacks early stimulation (in many cases he/she is locked in his/her home or room) and exposed to stressful situations other than hunger, including illness and violence, but there are also no educational programs that include them, critical preschool education is generally absent or if it exists, it is provided by untrained personnel. The interaction of all these elements leads to a negative potentiation of these factors, which contributes to a poor development of psychomotor and cognitive skills in the infant stage, resulting in inadequate conditions for the development of rational mental functions. The perspective of a malnourished child is that of an adult individual incapable of developing his or her potential as an adult in the family and in society, which contributes to preventing social mobility and upward mobility and contributes to reproducing the conditions of poverty. In other words, the vicious circle of poverty as a generator of misery and poverty in new generations will continue.

Stress, poverty and brain plasticity

One way to study stress in the laboratory is to separate newborn rats from their mothers. Separation is a major stressor for mothers, but neonates in particular are likely to feel abandoned, vulnerable and deprived of maternal warmth and nutrition The normal response of the body to a stressful situation is stimulation of the nervous system and endocrine system with increased production and release of hormones and neurotransmitters (cortisol, adrenaline, noradrenaline). This allows the body to respond metabolically to stressors and produce energy that ensures survival. However, while these hormones ensure survival, it has been seen that in continuously or chronically released, persistent stress, cortisol and the other hormones negatively affect brain development, especially the development of highly plastic anatomical brain structures such as the hippocampus, amygdala and frontal lobes. The effects of stress hormones reduce processes such as synaptogenesis, the formation of dendrites, which are necessary for synaptogenesis, and the development of neural connections and circuits in these brain structures. Processes related to memory, particularly working memory, are conducted in the hippocampus; it is also known that the hippocampus is connected to the frontal lobe, where executive processes such as decision-making take place. In other words, in order to make decisions we require memory ability. On the other hand, the amygdala takes part in emotions and is also interrelated with the hippocampus. It is therefore proposed that structural alterations of the hippocampus, amygdala or frontal lobe may affect processes such as working memory, the ability for self-regulation of emotions and decision making.

In fact, there are some studies that have looked at stressed children and compared them to non-stressed children. Stressed children have elevated levels of cortisol, epinephrine and norepinephrine compared to non-stressed children. In cognitive tests, children under stress were seen to perform poorly on tests assessing working memory, cognitive control of emotions, and language. Similarly, adults with a history of poverty perform poorly on tests of working memory, suggesting that this change may be permanent.

The question arises here: Is there a connection between poverty, chronic stress and cognitive changes in childhood? The answer is that there are many connections. Poverty is associated with socioeconomic stressors related to family income (unemployment, underemployment) that contribute to chronic stressors such as hunger, malnutrition, overcrowding and poor sanitary conditions that contribute to an increase in infectious diseases. Domestic violence, family dysfunctions, presence of delinquent relatives, children born and/or living in prison, school violence (bullying), violence in community environments (favelas, neighborhoods, communes, colonies) associated with common crime and/or related to drug trafficking. All these factors are persistent ingredients that create conditions of chronic stress that can be negative during early childhood when brain development is in full swing.

In many countries where misery and poverty afflict large sectors of the population, and probably supported by scientific evidence, feeding programs have been introduced in school restaurants that provide free meals to many low-income students, who are often sent by their parents motivated by the free food rather than by the educational offer. These initiatives, unfortunately, have been affected in the last two years by mandatory confinement, which is likely to be reflected in setbacks in social welfare indicators that had been achieved before the pandemic. Other factors, especially those related to multiple-cause violence, are still present and are likely to persist due to the inability of governments to sustain social welfare policies. This holds a bleak future for the adults of tomorrow, as social mobility and upward mobility are not possible, which favors the persistence of social differences and the gap between rich and poor, phenomena that have always existed but have been accentuated in the last century.

References.

Interested readers are encouraged to review the following documents.

- Olson, L., Chen, B., & Fishman, I. (2021). Neural correlates of socioeconomic status in early childhood: a systematic review of the literature. Child Neuropsychology, 27(3), 390-423.

- Ortiz-Andrellucchi, A., Peña Quintana, L., Albino Beñacar, A., Mönckeberg Barros, F., & Serra-Majem, L. (2006). Child malnutrition, health and poverty: intervention from a comprehensive program. Nutrición hospitalaria, 21(4), 533-541.

- Brown, J. L., & Pollitt, E. (1996). Malnutrition, poverty and intellectual development. Scientific American, 274(2), 38-43.

- Prado, E. L., & Dewey, K. G. (2014). Nutrition and brain development in early life. Nutrition reviews, 72(4), 267-284.

- Kempermann, G. (2019). Environmental enrichment, new neurons and the neurobiology of individuality. Nature Reviews Neuroscience, 20(4), 235-245.

- Moreno Fernández, R. D., Pedraza, C., & Gallo, M. (2013). Adult hippocampal neurogenesis and cognitive aging. Psychology

Writings (Internet), 6(3), 14-24.

- Bergado-Rosado, J. A., & Almaguer-Melian, W. (2000). Cellular mechanisms of neuroplasticity. Rev Neurol, 31(11), 1074-95.

THE FRONTAL LOBE IN TODAY'S SOCIETY

"Remember that politics, colonialism, imperialism and war also originate in the human brain."

Vilayanur Subramanian Ramachandran.

Indian-American neuroscientist.

D r. Rodolfo Linas, a world-renowned neurophysiologist, explained that large cities, especially his hometown Bogotá, lack frontal lobes. He used this metaphor to explain why cities were not developing as fast as they should be especially a cosmopolitan city like Bogota, strategically located on the American continent. The statement can be extended to the whole of today's society, as it can be said that the function of the social frontal lobe is deficient.

Why mention the frontal lobe? Because of the following, we humans refer to ourselves as superior rational beings. As "rational" beings, we have the ability to conduct complex mental processes such as judgment, reasoning, abstraction, acceptance of and compliance with norms and rules, self-criticism, and introspection. The part of the brain that controls such complex mental processes in humans is the frontal lobe. This brain structure is from the point of view of human evolution a young and prominent structure in most humans. But from the developmental point of view of each individual it is the one that develops more slowly and only reaches maturity in adulthood. The frontal lobe controls the older parts of the brain: the paleocerebrum and archicerebrum, structures responsible for regulating emotions on the one hand and on the other hand the basic instinctive life functions of an individual. The frontal lobe is the foundation of culture and probably its appearance was the engine that made human beings function as a social collective moving in the direction of development and progress.

In recent decades multiple social phenomena have put the stability of society in crisis: economic crises in different parts of the world, the presence of local and global terrorism, the growing traffic of illicit drugs, human trafficking, the violation of human rights, corruption at all levels in leading institutions of society, including state and religious institutions. This leads to the change of traditional values, in a certain way manipulated or promoted through mass media such as television, written media, internet, in many cases that induce and unify massive behaviors, usually of consumption, which have as a background purely commercial purposes. In all these problems the function of the brain and its higher abilities and its manipulation are an extremely critical point: we want to satisfy personal instincts over the collective welfare; we fail in the ability to plan, execute and make decisions of social impact at high economic, political or religious levels. This allows us to suspect serious failures in frontal lobe function and therefore in the individual's ability to think critically, to set up right judgments and to have the capacity to control the emotional and instinctive side. The result of all this is that in today's society there is a tendency to egocentrism, the hedonistic individual makes his needs take precedence over the needs of others. Manifestations of this are behaviors characterized by facilism, where the law of least effort and immediacy prevails, with the pursuit of accelerated results without planning or foresight of consequences, and above all, often applying the maxim that the end justifies the means, whether or not socially accepted. All these behaviors of the individual are reflected in the social environment, this environment can be your home, your neighborhood on a small scale, but on a large scale your country or the world: corruption, violence and violation of human rights are among others, reflections of this problem.

Brain, politics, and society: neuropolitics

Politics is an activity in which a group of citizens make a series of decisions that look for the good of a community. In this sense, all human beings belonging to a social group are political by nature and should be able to make judgments and make decisions based on them. There are several investigations conducted in recent decades aimed at understanding human political behavior and the participation of brain areas in this behavior. Neuroimaging techniques in general have supplied information to understand how our political brain works. It has been shown that both society and institutions can influence the individual to assume a political behavior.

Right brain vs. left brain.

A recent study carried out in groups of people with either conservative or liberal tendencies has shown that people with liberal tendencies have greater activity in the anterior region of the cingulate cortex, an area that is related to conflict resolution, recognition of the facial expression of others and assessment of the pleasure or displeasure that a particular activity can produce, among other functions. In the case of individuals with extreme liberal behaviors, there is an increase in the gray matter of this area. In the group of extreme conservative individuals, a greater volume of gray matter was seen in the right amygdala, an area related to the expression of emotions, including the response to fear, response to sexual hormones, and reaction to invasion of personal space. Another study showed that when individuals were exposed to threatening stimuli (stimuli that can be images or sounds), those who responded physiologically to threats more intensely were individuals who professed more conservative political ideas (ideas of defense of the state, of the death penalty, criminalization of abortion). Those who responded less to threatening stimuli presented more open ideas (empathy with migrants, rejection of the death penalty).

Mirror neurons and politics.

Mirror neurons are a group of neurons in the prefrontal region that are activated when we perform an action or when we see another individual perform an action. It is proposed that they are the neural basis of empathy, that is, the ability to feel what others feel, that is, to put ourselves in the shoes of others. Understanding the pain, suffering or happiness of others. We feel sadness if our interlocutor looks sad or cries and we laugh if the other looks happy or laughs. These mirror neurons are connected to the limbic system, which activates our emotional responses. Some researchers declare that in politics, empathy in voters is fundamental. This is achieved thanks to messages, speeches and images that awaken feelings, enthusiasm and optimism. A study conducted in 2004 showed that when presenting the image of a candidate who was in the middle of a campaign, the brain areas where the mirror neurons are found increased their activity in those people who had greater affinity with that candidate. A control study conducted months later on these same people showed that this activity was reduced. The researchers interpreted this as the effect of the negative campaigning that candidates face, which ultimately affects the voter. Many candidates who appear as the hope of a society lose popularity thanks to negative campaigns against them.

Genes and policy

Since the 1980s, twin studies have been conducted to determine the influence of genes on political behavior or decisions. The results show that the interaction between genes and environment are key in defining political behavior. Several studies have shown that behaviors such as altruism, empathy, cooperation, and the ability to assume risks are largely inherited behaviors. The presence of genes coding for a certain type of dopamine receptor (DRD4) has been linked as an element that predisposes people who possess it to have a certain political tendency. Dopamine participates in the control of movements and its alteration leads to motor diseases such as Parkinson's disease, but dopamine is also involved in the generation of emotions and thoughts. Love and empathy depend on dopamine. Alterations in dopamine function at this level generate diverse pathologies that include schizophrenia, a disorder in which the individual's ability for judgment and interpretation of reality is affected. Given that political behavior involves more than one of these behaviors, it is suggested that in a certain way politics would be dependent on our genetic load.

The current results supply data that reinforce the idea of the presence of two major functions of the central nervous system by two defined brain structures: the limbic system and the frontal lobe. The limbic system allows us to recognize threats and guarantees our survival: feeding, recognition of environmental threats, regulation of sexual drives to guarantee conservation of the species (sense of power, sense of belonging, territoriality, dominance, sexuality). The frontal area allows us to control the emotional limbic part and allows us to analyze, plan and project actions, which is called executive function (planning, execution, legislation, projection, agreement, dialogue, tolerance).

In politics, on many occasions it is a matter of manipulating the affective part by presenting the voter with negative aspects of the political opponents (they are labeled as dictators, corrupt, criminals, terrorists) and the threats that can be presented (poverty, misery, communism, underdevelopment). This is done through language (the skilled speaker has greater influence), the mass media (commercials with tricks, dubious information and ambiguous slogans, manipulated polls, televised debates that may be biased) where a large number of voters can be influenced, who often do not have the possibility of analyzing the information.

Although there is scientific information obtained in the last decades, so far it is not conclusive and raises new current questions: Does growing up in a family with conservative or liberal tendencies modify the brain structure, can physical or psychological traumas modify the political thinking of a leader (think of the Stockholm syndrome), can the leader of the extreme left or right, who polarizes a community, a society or a country, modify the brain structure of his electors, and if so, can he modify the brain structure of his voters?

The increase in information about how the brain functions in relation to decision making and political behavior has allowed many researchers to speak of a new area in neuroscience: neuropolitics. There are several articles and books dealing with multiple aspects of this new topic. The questions that arise around this topic are broad and governments are interested in creating or have created research departments in this area, which opens ethical discussions due to the possible manipulation of this information.

The frontal lobe and money: neuroeconomics

A topic that has begun to develop in the area of neuroscience is neuroeconomics, a topic that is very much in tune with the times of global economic crisis in which we live. The central hypothesis of this line of research is that economics (as well as politics) is an area where the activity of the nervous system, especially the frontal lobe, is fundamental. Economic decision making, from the individual level that involves the purchase of a product to the collective level that includes guiding the economy of a region or a country, involves the ability to analyze, the ability to make judgments, the ability to calculate risks, the ability to foresee complications, to be able to propose solutions, and includes intuition itself. These are all activities controlled by the frontal lobe but interacting with other systems. If the frontal lobe fails due to immaturity (as in the child or adolescent) or damage (Phineas Gage case) these decisions or processes are contaminated by the activity of old areas from the evolutionary point of view and that control the instincts, the search for pleasure, survival. Probably in cases of altered frontal lobe function it is not the reason derived from the frontal lobe function that decides, but our primitive brain (the limbic system) that takes command to satisfy the needs of the instinctive part. Sometimes we take reasons guided by the stomach or by the heart and not by reason, as already in the 17th century the French philosopher and mathematician Blaise Pascal suspected when he said that "The heart has reasons that reason does not know". Sometimes decisions are affected or contaminated by what we see, smell or feel, and these sensations are initially projected to the instinctive brain.

Many aspects related to dysfunction or alteration in the function of the frontal lobe are visible both individually and collectively and do not discriminate, i.e. they manifest themselves in any individual, from the anonymous citizen to the highest ranking leader: aggressiveness, lack of respect for social norms and institutions, intolerance, inability to make correct decisions, lack of planning, decision making oriented to satisfy basic personal interests and needs or those of particular groups. Corruption, bribery, illicit enrichment, evasion, abuse of power, are just examples of how decision making sometimes goes against what is socially acceptable and satisfies the individual's desires. This determines behaviors that can be criminal and represent a risk for the economic and political stability of a society. Currently, there is a kind of exacerbation of these phenomena, why is this happening and what is the cause? There is no clear answer, but there are some hypotheses that try to explain it. One interesting theory is that of mirror neurons, which says that there are areas of the brain that are activated when we perform an action (eating, crying or laughing, for example), which are also activated when we see another person performing the same action, hence the name mirror neurons. When a person performs a socially impermissible activity: robbery, rape, assault, kidnapping, and sees the suffering it causes, areas of the brain related to suffering (mirror neurons) are activated in the normal individual, which forces the individual to control himself and generate feelings of guilt, compassion, solidarity, as the case may be. In a sick person, especially those whose frontal lobe structure or function is affected, this does not happen. An example of this is in people with schizophrenia or in people affected by neurodegenerative diseases: senile dementia, Alzheimer's disease, etc. However, in cases where the victim is not directly visible to the perpetrator (bankrupts and white-collar robbers, drug users and drug traffickers, family members of kidnappers and extortionists, etc.) more complex processes are needed on the part of the perpetrator, involving deeper analysis and reflection (ultimately frontal lobe maturation). These processes depend on a maturation of the frontal lobe which in turn depends on biological factors, but fundamentally on the environment through education, family influence and the social environment, which is not always present and not all of us have. An increasingly poor enriched environment, with short, incomplete and distorted messages (education, media, ambiguous leaders or without moral authority) can make the majority of the population unable to perceive the suffering of the other, unable to generate feelings of guilt and may even become sympathetic not with the victim but with the victimizer. The war in Iraq is wrong, but it is not in my territory, or it was in defense of freedom and democracy; there is discrimination, but it does not affect me, it is not me, or it is not in my space. This is a current phenomenon and is nowadays incorporated in the term desensitization. Although it may be a term applied incorrectly, since desensitization implies prior sensitization and apparently we never activate mirror neurons for certain actions or phenomena, which implies that sensitization to the experiences and/or suffering of others is never generated, in the end we ignore it and therefore we are indifferent.

The conclusion that can be reached after this brief reflection is that the function of the frontal lobe is fundamental in the human being and that this is reflected in society, which in turn feeds back the maturation of the individual through the family, education and the different artistic, sporting and scientific social manifestations. Given that there are collective symptoms reflecting inadequate frontal lobe function in modern society, we are faced with two possibilities: The first is that today's society has a very young frontal lobe that is in full development (individuals who are maturing emotionally and intellectually later and later), which is hopeful because we can shape its development and hope for a better future. The more troubling possibility is that we are part of an aging society with a clear and progressive deterioration of its frontal lobe, in which case the prognosis is guarded.

Let's hope that as humanity our brain is that of a child, evolving and hopefully, if we have a positive enriched environment, that every day that goes by it will be better. Otherwise, we would be with a schizophrenic adult frontal lobe or Alzheimer's, which would be terrible because every day we are going to be worse.

In light of this, neurosciences cannot propose solutions as they primarily seek to understand the processes. Solutions or treatment go from the individual to the collective, and involve sectors of the economy, politics, the media, educational institutions, society as a whole. It is common in medicine for the empirical to precede the scientific. The plants used by Aboriginal people to treat various diseases, or grandmother's "remedy", have been the basis for the production of diverse types of modern drugs. This means that society in many cases has been able to diagnose its illnesses and look for the "remedy" or doctor to help control them. In this sense, neurosciences are supplying elements to know why we do what we do and if we are doing the things we should or want to do. And it is quite possible that society itself will come up with the magic recipe or the doctor (leader) who will take on its treatment.

The frontal lobe and morality: Neuroethics

In everyday life we use the term morality, or its counterpart immorality and we act accordingly and are judged by society in these terms. But what is morality? When is something moral and when is it not? How did the concept of morality originate? Why are our actions controlled by morality? These and other questions are what Dr. Patricia Churchland, a world-renowned neurophilosopher, tries to answer in a book entitled "Braintrust".

For Dr. Churchland, the origin of morality has a biological foundation that exists in the brain. In the brain there are a series of circuits that determine the creation of affective bonds and the development of feelings of trust between individuals. For this development of affection and trust, interaction with others, i.e., social behavior, is fundamental. Therefore, an early key moment in the development of morality was the ability to care for others. In mammals it was no longer enough to have instinctive mechanisms that guaranteed self-preservation, mechanisms were also developed that guaranteed the survival of young offspring or incapacitated adults and thus the survival of the species. To guarantee this, especially to protect the offspring, biological changes were developed that guaranteed the initial formation of the individual inside the mother, a stage known as the prenatal stage; this takes place in the uterus in the case of mammals. The time of intrauterine development varies depending on the species. After the period of intrauterine formation and maturation comes the birth and the encounter of the offspring with a hostile environment. During the first days, months or years post-partum the new individual has the protection and maternal nourishment, it depends on a fundamental exocrine gland the mammary gland which allows to coin the term mammalian. The mammary gland is the structure that allows contact and communication between mother and child, contact that is kept during the lactation period and that will be necessary to ensure the nutrition and proper development of the new individual, especially psychomotor development. Thus, during this breastfeeding period, some skills are developed in the infant.

The ability to recognize others (maternal faces and those of close relatives, familiar voices, household smells) and the ability to recognize the psychological state of others, whether of well-being or discomfort (joy, tranquility, anger, sadness) and to respond according to what he/she perceives is generated. The child, in the case of humans, identifies parents and relatives and their mood through gestures or tone of voice and responds accordingly, generating feelings of empathy and or rejection. Empathy is a feeling that involves a sense of well-being, a sense of security and a sense of protection in the child, which guarantees the creation of trust and initial family bonds and later social relationships.

Oxytocin and trusting relationships

In the history of humanity, the formation of the family group guaranteed constant protection, food and care among individuals. The union of family groups further strengthened these benefits, but also generated clashes between individuals. From social interaction arose the need to regulate individual interactions. For example, to solve problems that would guarantee the well-being of individuals and the stability of the community; to guarantee the fair distribution of food; to solve territorial disputes; the concept of property, crime and punishment was also generated. One of these punishments was social isolation (ostracism). The individual isolated from the community is deprived of the benefits that the community supplies and would be defenseless against environmental threats, which generates extreme stress in the punished individual. Separation and exclusion cause pain that can lead to death, a phenomenon that has been described in experiments on animal species.

Behaviors tending to reinforce social coexistence activities (moral behaviors) are reinforced through the learning of social practices that is carried out permanently: using positive reinforcement to stimulate behaviors or negative reinforcement to eliminate undesired behaviors, using different mechanisms such as imitation in children, trial and error, or by analogy in adolescents and adults.

What elements of the nervous system take part in these individual behaviors that extend to the group? In all this development the role of the central nervous system is fundamental and in particular the role of a neurotransmitter is key: oxytocin. Oxytocin is a chemical substance produced in the brain, an ancient chemical in the evolutionary chain, i.e., it is not exclusive to human beings. Oxytocin is produced in an area of the ancient brain, the hypothalamus, and from there it is released in a central gland close to the hypothalamus at the base of the brain: the neurohypophysis, from there oxytocin goes into the bloodstream to be distributed throughout the body. Oxytocin has multiple functions: it promotes tissue growth and repair, takes part in childbirth by stimulating muscle contractions in the uterus, lowers the pain threshold, reduces cortisol levels, lowers blood pressure, and has the effect of reducing anxiety, i.e., it reduces stress levels. These processes ultimately favor the rapprochement between individuals, social interaction, participates in falling in love and in general favors the establishment of relationships of empathy and familiarity. Its release and action allow the reduction of aggressive attitudes and the development of behaviors such as trust between each other, which is necessary to develop affective bonds, initially between parents and children, then between families, groups and society. From this, social institutions and ultimately morality appear.

Moral values, argues Dr. Churchland, have their origin in the care of offspring, a behavior common to all mammals. From this point on, circuits and brain chemicals are consolidated, inducing mammals to strive not only for their own self-preservation (survival), but also for that of those close to them: offspring initially, partners, relatives and so on in ever-widening circles of care. Companionship and protection generate feelings of well-being, security and pleasure. Therefore, morality is based on processes related to:

1. Caring. Related to family ties and caring for their welfare.

2. Recognition of others and their psychological state. This is linked to the ability to evaluate and predict their behavior.

3. Learning of social practices. In the family and in the social environment by reinforcement, by imitation, by trial and error, by analogy.

4. Problem solving in a social context. Distribution of scarce food, disputes over colonized land, penalties and punishments for crimes, among others.

Responding to feelings of pleasure (social inclusion and protection) and pain (social exclusion) the brain adjusts its circuits according to local customs. One social group may have different moral behaviors than another social group developed in a different geographical environment. With this it can be affirmed that care, conscience and moral institution and morality are associated and reflect progressive levels of complexity that would have a biological basis. As social groups evolve, social interaction and its various aspects can be modified. This is reflected in many of the world's current issues related to conflict resolution, peacekeeping, development of defense programs, development of wealth distribution programs and policies, discussions around the concept of social justice, among others.

Another neuroscientist who has investigated these aspects is Dr. Paul Zach, who calls oxytocin the moral molecule. He argues that prosperous and developed countries have individuals with a higher degree of trust than those that are not developed. In such countries there are more economic transactions, probably due to higher levels of trust among the population, which would explain the level of development. He proposes that the use of oxytocin could favor the development of poor nations. These ideas are framed within a new area which is neuroeconomics.

But extending this proposal to other fields, we could think that aggressiveness and violence could also be related to oxytocin to the extent that social violence is more frequent in undeveloped countries where social problems such as unwanted pregnancies, teenage pregnancies, child abandonment, lack of breastfeeding in the first years of life, maternal and child malnutrition and social stress in general are more frequent. Studies show that stress, malnutrition and testosterone are factors that inhibit oxytocin production. This would generate a continuous vicious circle of mistrust, stress, insecurity, violence. This would prevent the generation of trust and family ties, the basis of morality. Reducing factors that inhibit oxytocin production (stress, malnutrition) could favor states of well-being, tranquility and trust among individuals. Breaking this vicious circle may require the participation of many political, economic, educational, religious, scientific areas and institutions. Of course, all the participants leading these areas must produce enough oxytocin to be able to generate ideas that guarantee a global and not partial social change.

Brain Plasticity, Learning and Society: Neuroeducation

Brain plasticity, also known as neuroplasticity, refers to the brain's ability to adapt and change its structure in response to experience. This is done through the formation of new synaptic contacts between neurons, a process called synaptogenesis. These contacts can be changed by increasing in number when there are constant stimuli or decreasing when the stimuli disappear or diminish. Thanks to synaptogenesis, neuronal circuits can be strengthened, new circuits can be formed or underutilized circuits can disappear. It is proposed that synaptic plasticity is a process that plays a fundamental role in learning and memory, as well as in the recovery of altered functions after brain injury.

Education is a process aimed at developing the psychomotor abilities of the individual, guaranteeing his or her capacity to interact with the environment, interpret it and adapt to the changes that arise, ensuring individual and collective survival. Basic neuronal processes that include attention, motivation, memory and learning are fundamental in education. All these processes are the basis for the development of formal mental functions such as judgment, reasoning, intelligence, among others. In this sense, both formal and informal education stimulate brain plasticity. Studies in animal models and clinical studies in humans have shown that performing intellectually stimulating activities, such as reading, learning a new skill or solving puzzles, can help improve cognitive function and increase brain plasticity. Physical exercise, social interaction and a healthy diet may also contribute to brain plasticity.

Although there is controversy about whether it is valid to extrapolate directly to the real world the results reported in the scientific literature obtained in experimental subjects and under controlled conditions, it is important that schools recognize the role of the brain in learning and design educational experiences that promote brain development and functioning. This should include creating school environments enriched with a variety of learning activities, stimulating and motivating the development of new skills, and providing opportunities to combine intellectual academic activity with physical activity. Likewise, the educational system must guarantee a minimum of social and emotional well-being for students.

It is important to keep in mind that the brain's ability to change and adapt can diminish with age, and that certain lifestyle factors, such as chronic stress, can negatively affect brain plasticity. However, research suggests that it is never too late to adopt healthy behaviors that can support brain plasticity and cognitive function.

Brain and leadership

The topic of leadership is an extremely complex but relevant area in species where their survival depends on groups. Leadership is a topic that has been and is studied in the animal realm (both invertebrate and vertebrate animals) but is relevant to the understanding of human groups.

From biology and zoology, a discipline appeared: ethology, an area that shed much light on the biological forces that drive leadership and its role in group cohesion. Perhaps the most important function of leadership in a given species is to ensure the survival of that species, through the coordination of tasks between individuals and group cohesion that ensures the survival of the species (foraging, mobility, exploration, protection from risk) and its conservation (through procreation).

The process involves natural selection, which usually allows the healthy males of a species to reproduce, relegating all those individuals that do not have the physical capacity to survive. From the biological point of view, it is apparently fundamental to set in motion neuroendocrine circuits, which form the primitive brain, involved in diverse functions including visual, motor, behavioral (aggressiveness) and reproductive (pheromones, sex hormones) and which are activated under specific conditions. The male leader exercises control over his group and the mechanisms to exercise his leadership are related to the use of force and instilling fear in his group and in front of other groups of the same or distinct species.

At the human level, these basic biological mechanisms are also employed, but they are not the only ones. In addition to the use of physical force resulting from primitive brain activity, the higher mental activities of the neocerebrum are involved, where the function of the frontal lobe is essential (determining processes that include language, judgment, reasoning, decision making, etc.); to generate mechanisms of persuasion where language is involved to transmit ideas.

However, in the subject of leadership and in the group we always find two dynamic actors: the leader and the followers. The leader must possess special characteristics that give him an advantage over the other members of the group (age, physical capacity, socioeconomic status, gender, etc.), but others allow him to be able to exert influence over the other members of the group and that depends on his superior mental functions, including mastery of language, ability to associate ideas, ability to analyze and synthesize, ability to persuade, among others. This leadership capacity can produce positive results or negative results, which can determine the prosperity and life of the leader and his followers (analyze the case of leadership in historical characters such as Jesus, Gandi, Martyr Luther King) or can have negative effects that lead to the failure and death of the leader and his followers (Charles Manson, Adolf Hitler, Jim Jones).The decisions made by the leader when declaring a war, inducing fights for sports, religious or racial affinities, among others, depend on the characteristics of the leader, his history, his experiences and his thinking, which will affect his followers. The followers, on the other hand, as a group of individuals, have special characteristics (emergent characteristics proper to their belonging to the group with which they have common interests) that the individual does not have when he is outside that group. The actions of the individual (father or son of a family) are different when he acts within the family, than when he acts in a political, religious, sports, cultural or antisocial group. In these cases, individual responsibility is diluted in the collective and patterns of behavior are created that are usually specific to the group. The leader can manipulate his followers and exploit them to fulfill personal aims, or he can function as a guide to achieve a collective benefit. The leader's character, derived from its adequate development, neurological and mental maturity, will be determinant for the destiny of the group. Alterations in brain development, structure and function, due to multiple causes (neuropsychiatric diseases, drug use and abuse, after-effects of trauma and violence, among many others) can alter the leader's character and orientation. But these same characteristics apply to the followers and will determine passive and conformist attitudes of the group or a more initiative-taking and critical attitude. Given the current social crises of all kinds and the feeling of absence of true leaders, this is a field that needs much more study and a transdisciplinary approach that includes not only psychologists, neurologists, psychiatrists and/or neuroscientists, but also human and social sciences in general. The subject of study should not be exclusively, as it has been so far, that of the leader and leadership, but should involve the study of followers, which, in a world where social upheavals are increasingly frequent, can contribute to the understanding and solution of many of the current crises.

References.

Interested readers are encouraged to review the following documents.

- Cook, R., Bird, G., Catmur, C., Press, C., & Heyes, C. (2014). Mirror neurons: from origin to function. Behavioral and brain sciences, 37(2), 177-192.

- Krastev, S., McGuire, J. T., McNeney, D., Kable, J. W., Stolle, D., Gidengil, E., & Fellows, L. K. (2016). Do political and economic choices rely on common neural substrates? A systematic review of the emerging neuropolitics literature. Frontiers in psychology, 7, 264.

- Serra, D. (2021). Decision-making: from neuroscience to neuroeconomics-an overview. Theory and Decision, 91(1), 1-80.

- Schreiber, D. (2017). Neuropolitics: Twenty years later. Politics and the Life Sciences, 36(2), 114-131.

- Glimcher, P. W., & Rustichini, A. (2004). Neuroeconomics: the consilience of brain and decision. Science, 306(5695), 447-452.

- Ramos, K. M., Grady, C., Greely, H. T., Chiong, W., Eberwine, J., Farahany, N. A., ... & Koroshetz, W. J. (2019). The NIH BRAIN initiative: Integrating neuroethics and neuroscience. Neuron, 101(3), 394-398.

- Goswami, U. (2009). Mind, brain, and literacy: Biomarkers as usable knowledge for education. Mind, Brain, and Education, 3(3), 176-184.

EXOBRAIN: ¿GLOBAL BRAIN?

"The more you think about and interact with other people, the more you realize that it is untenable to privilege your interests over theirs."

Steven Pinker.

Canadian neuroscientist.

With the advance of technology, human beings have become dependent on it and even create relationships of extreme man-machine interdependence, in which it is impossible to conceive of the individual without such symbiosis. Since the middle of the 20th century, some words have been created to describe such relationships. One of these novel words is "Cyborg" (formed from the fusion of the words "cybernetics" and "organism"), a term used to describe a creature composed of organic substances and mechanical or artificial elements, in which this symbiosis, the individual maintains the human form. So, an individual who uses a cardiac pacemaker, cochlear implant, or knee prosthesis is a cyborg.

Another term used is lobster, which is used to describe individuals with a synthetic shell and a living inner organism. In this case the exoskeleton can take on non-human forms. Thus, a man in an automobile, motorcycle, or airplane is a lobster, an individual with new capabilities. But the man-machine relationship can not only be individual; it can also be collective. Thus, the existence of living collectives in artificial mega-constructions such as skyscrapers and mega-cities is proposed. Streets, railroads, means of communication create a network that forms a complex organism made up of interconnected living beings.

Analogous to the proposal of the human-machine relationship, there is an interesting proposal in the area of neurosciences, which suggests that in addition to the individual brain, there is a brain external to the individual: the exo-brain. According to this proposal, our brain depends on or requires an external shell that allows it to reach its largest functionality. This proposal comes from the social sciences, not from biology, and was put forward by Dr. Roger Bartra, a Mexican anthropologist and sociologist.

For Dr. Bartra, the brain and a manifestation of its function: consciousness, can only be explained by referring to the term exocerebrum.

The exocerebrum is defined as the cultural prosthesis that arises from society and interacts with the brain of the individual; from this interaction emerges consciousness. This cultural prosthesis is represented by language, symbols, myths and in general the knowledge of cultural transmission. Without these elements, the biological brain and the consciousness can hardly develop fully. However, there is much controversy in this regard; there are extreme positions in which, on the one hand, it is argued that consciousness is basically an emergent property of the brain, and on the other hand, there are those who argue that consciousness does not exist and that it is only a construct of philosophers.

However, analyzing this proposal in detail could help explain certain normal and pathological phenomena. We have the ability to acquire language, but this only occurs in social practice. We have the ability for spatial and mathematical abstraction, but this only occurs with interaction with the environment and education. Under normal conditions, the influence of the environment on brain function may not be so clear, but in pathological conditions, this may be more evident when aberrant or abnormal conditions are created. Take schizophrenia, for example. In schizophrenia, genetic and biological factors have been invoked as determinants, specifically an imbalance of the dopaminergic system in the frontal lobe. However, in the case of the paranoid schizophrenic with megalomaniac ideation, the question arises as to whether the individual who hallucinates about being Napoleon, Bolivar or Churchill, would hallucinate about being these characters without earlier education. Would a schizophrenic in China hallucinate about these characters or would he hallucinate about Mao Tse Tung, Confucius, Lao Tse? In this case the society (the cultural exocerebro) interacts with the individual in whose brain there is a pathological disorder, and a response is generated, a behavior is created. But the influence can be inverse, the individual brain can act on a part or the whole society to generate a collective behavior that can be positive or negative, depending on the perspective from which you look at it. In the same way that a neuron or a group of neurons in a "normal" brain can originate an epileptic seizure or a brilliant idea. Think of Hitler as an individual and the National Socialist movement in Germany; Benito Mussolini, Joseph Stalin, Mao Tse Tung. The influence of an individual on a sick society -a collective in crisis- can be harmful. However, the influence can also be positive: Jesus, Mohammed, Gandhi, Martin Luther King, Nelson Mandela and so many others who have inspired constructive, progressive and tolerant behavior in a collective.

Although it is difficult to refute or accept such a proposal, it is key to understand that knowledge and truth can be approached with a transdisciplinary view. On the other hand, it allows us to reflect on how we are shaped by the environment that surrounds us, how we interact, and how we are dependent. One of these elements of the external environment of recent appearance, technology, can lead us to new forms of thought and reality: transhumanism, exo-brain, cyborgs are just a foretaste of the future.

References.

Interested readers are encouraged to review the following documents.

- Kingsbury, L., & Hong, W. (2020). A multi-brain framework for social interaction. Trends in neurosciences, 43(9), 651-666.

- Chen, P., & Hong, W. (2018). Neural circuit mechanisms of social behavior. Neuron, 98(1), 16-30.

- Tognoli, E., Guzman, G. C. D., & Kelso, J. A. (2011). Interacting humans and the dynamics of their social brains. In Advances in Cognitive Neurodynamics (II) (pp. 139-143). Springer, Dordrecht.

- Porcelli, S., Van Der Wee, N., van der Werff, S., Aghajani, M., Glennon, J. C., van Heukelum, S., ... & Serretti, A. (2019). Social brain, social dysfunction and social withdrawal. Neuroscience & Biobehavioral Reviews, 97, 10-33.

- Georgieff, N., & Jeannerod, M. (1998). Beyond consciousness of external reality: a "who" system for consciousness of action and self-consciousness. Consciousness and cognition, 7(3), 465-477.

- Bartra, R. (2017). The exocerebrum: a hypothesis about consciousness. Ludus Vitalis, 13(23), 103-115.